Rainforests at Risk

Jen Green

Chrysalis Children's Books

First published in the UK in 2003 by
Chrysalis Children's Books
An imprint of Chrysalis Books Group Plc
The Chrysalis Building, Bramley Road,
London W10 6SP

Paperback edition first published in 2005
Copyright © Chrysalis Books Group Plc 2003

ISBN 1 84138 715 0 (hb)
ISBN 1 84458 247 7 (pb)

British Library Cataloguing in Publication
Data for this book is available from the
British Library.

Editorial Manager: Joyce Bentley
Picture Researcher: Terry Forshaw
Produced by Tall Tree Ltd
Designer: Ed Simkins
Editor: Kate Phelps
Consultant: Michael Rand

Printed in China

Some of the more unfamiliar words used in this book
are explained in the glossary on page 31.

Photo Credits:
Front cover (main), J. C. Vincent/Still Pictures; front cover
(clockwise from top left), Mark Edwards/Still Pictures; Robert
Pickett/Ecoscene; Herbert Giradet/Still Pictures;
Cooper/Ecoscene; Tom Brakefield/Corbis; 1, Mark Edwards/Still
Pictures; 2, Robert Pickett/Ecoscene; 4, Cyril Ruoso/Still Pictures;
5(t), J. C. Vincent/Still Pictures; 5(b), Herbert Giradet/Still
Pictures; 7, J. J. Alcalay/Still Pictures; 9(t), Luiz C. Marigo/Still
Pictures; 9(b), Simon Grove/Ecoscene; 11(t), Chinch
Gryniewicz/Ecoscene; 11(b), Mark Edwards/Still Pictures; 12,
Mike Kolloffel/Still Pictures; 13(t), Robert Pickett/Papilio; 13(b),
Ecoscene; 14, J. C. Vincent/Still Pictures; 15(t), Wayne
Lawler/Ecoscene; 15(b), George Disario/Corbis; 16, Wolfgang
Kaehler/Corbis; 17(t), Frans Rombout/Bubbles; 17(b), Patrick
Chalmers/Reuters; 18, Sally Morgan/Ecoscene; 19(t), Ron
Chapple/Getty Images; 19(b), Sally Morgan/Ecoscene; 20,
Michael Gunther/Still Pictures; 21(t), Tom Brakefield/Corbis;
21(b), Gary Buss/Getty Images; 22, Herbert Giradet/Still
Pictures; 23(t), Adam Woolfitt/Corbis; 23(b), Brigitte Marcon-
Bios/Still Pictures; 24, Nigel Dickinson/Still Pictures; 25(t), Mark
Edwards/Still Pictures; 25(b), Klein/Hubert/Still Pictures; 26(t),
Kim Heacox/Still Pictures; 26(b), Mark Edwards/Still Pictures;
27(t), Robert Henno/Still Pictures; 27(b), Cooper/Ecoscene; 28,
Roland Seitre/Still Pictures; 29, Harwood/Ecoscene; 30, Cyril
Ruoso/Still Pictures; 31, J. J. Alcalay/Still Pictures; back cover,
Klein/Hubert/Still Pictures

Contents

Forests in peril

Imagine being in a huge forest with mighty tree trunks all around. High above your head, the dense leaves screen out most of the light. The air is warm and clammy. You can hear the sound of monkeys and birds in the treetops.

Rainforests are amazingly rich in wildlife. They cover just a small fraction of Earth's surface (about six per cent), yet they are home to two-thirds of all the species (different types) of animals and plants found on land.

▼ Most monkeys and apes are forest creatures. These orang-utans live in the rainforests of Indonesia.

You might think people would respect and protect these beautiful places. In fact, Earth's rainforests are disappearing fast. People are cutting down the trees for timber or clearing forests to make way for farms, mines and towns. However, it's not too late to save the rainforests. Forest people and many countries around the world are now working together to protect the remaining forests. We can all help.

LOOK CLOSER

Experts think that only about ten per cent of all the animals and plants that live in rainforests have so far been identified. Hundreds of new species are found and named each year.

▲ This logger is cutting down an area of rainforest in Cameroon in Africa. The ancient forests can be destroyed in just a few days using modern machinery such as chainsaws.

◀ At the Earth Summit in Brazil in 1992, representatives from countries all over the world met with rainforest people to try to work out ways to save the forests.

The rainforests

R ainforests are so-called because rain falls there almost every day. These lush forests receive at least 200 cm of rainfall annually. Several different types of rainforest exist around the world.

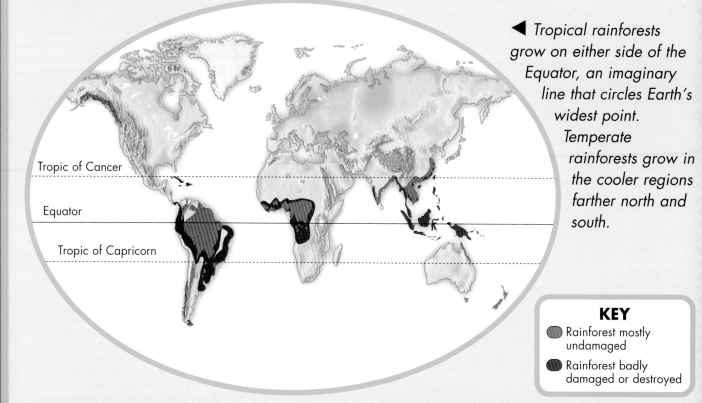

◀ Tropical rainforests grow on either side of the Equator, an imaginary line that circles Earth's widest point. Temperate rainforests grow in the cooler regions farther north and south.

Tropic of Cancer

Equator

Tropic of Capricorn

KEY
Rainforest mostly undamaged
Rainforest badly damaged or destroyed

Not all rainforests are the same. The best known are tropical rainforests, which grow near the Equator that marks Earth's widest point. The Sun beats down fiercely in the tropics, and the weather is hot and steamy all year round. The world's largest tropical rainforest is the Amazon region of South America. Huge tropical rainforests also grow in West Africa and Southeast Asia.

Emergents

Canopy

Understorey

Forest floor

◀ *Each layer, or storey, in the rainforest is home to particular types of animals and plants.*

Rainforest trees are like tall buildings with different layers, or storeys. High above the ground, the trees branch to form a dense, leafy layer called the canopy. The tallest trees, called emergents, rise above the canopy. The leafy canopy absorbs most of the sunlight and water, so the understorey below is drier and shady. Minibeasts and furry mammals search for food on the forest floor.

LOOK CLOSER

Rainforests also grow in the temperate zones north and south of the tropics. The climate is cooler there but still wet all year round. Mosses and ferns coat the trees in the Otway Ranges in Australia, shown here. Large temperate rainforests also grow in western North America, New Zealand, Chile and Japan.

Forest life

Rainforests are special places because of the huge variety of living things found there. This variety of wildlife is known as biodiversity. All the animals and plants of the rainforests depend on one another for survival.

The relationships between all the living things in the rainforest can be shown as a food chain. At the base of the chain are plants. The flowers, leaves and fruits of plants are eaten by animals such as insects, parrots and monkeys. In turn these are eaten by predators (hunters) such as eagles and big cats.

Eagles are carnivores (meat-eaters)

Parrots and monkeys are herbivores (plant-eaters)

▶ This diagram shows part of the food chain in the Amazon rainforest.

Leaves, fruit and flowers form the base of the food chain

Even a small patch of rainforest contains an amazing variety of life. Scientists have found 1500 types of plants, 400 types of birds and 150 different butterflies in an area just six km square.

When animals die, their bodies are broken down by insects, fungi and tiny organisms called bacteria. Animal and plant remains help to fertilise the soil so that more plants can grow, and so the cycle of life begins again. Forest soils do not contain many nutrients because the huge numbers of plants take all the nourishment.

▼ *Animal and plant remains rot quickly in the hot, damp conditions in rainforests. Fungi help to break down these remains.*

Life-givers

The world's rainforests cover only a small proportion of Earth's surface, but they help to support life over a much larger area. Forest trees help top up levels of oxygen in the atmosphere, which all animals need to survive.

Rainforests affect the climate of the surrounding region by increasing rainfall. Here's how it works. When rain falls, tree roots soak it up from the soil. The moisture travels up the tree and is slowly released from the leaves as water vapour. Water vapour forms clouds, which later shed rain, so the water is recycled again.

Sun

Water evaporates from the plants to form clouds

Rain falls from clouds

Plants absorb water through their roots

River

▶ Due to the intense heat from the Sun, the moisture in tropical rainforests is rapidly recycled, helping plants there to grow more quickly than anywhere else in the world.

Water evaporates from the river by the Sun's heat

All the oxygen in Earth's atmosphere is released by plants as they make their own food using energy from sunlight. The green leaves of plants gather this energy and use it to change carbon dioxide gas and water into food. This amazing process is called photosynthesis.

▼ Rainforest trees form a dark green blanket that absorbs heat and sunlight. The forest acts like an air-conditioning system, keeping the air cooler for thousands of kilometres around and releasing huge amounts of cooling water vapour.

CLOSE TO HOME

Trees and other plants help to balance the gases in the air around us. They absorb carbon dioxide and give off oxygen. Trees from rainforests (and other forests like the one shown here) play an important part in this process but can no longer do so if they are cut down.

Forest people

As well as animals and plants, the world's rainforests are also home to hundreds of people. The forests provide them with food, medicine, clothes and materials to build houses.

Forest people hunt animals and grow crops in ways that do not destroy the forest. They kill birds, monkeys, deer and pigs but take only what they need for food. They burn small patches of forest to grow fruit and vegetables, then allow the forest to grow back again.

◀ *Forest people use blowpipes and arrows to kill animals. If the forests are cut down, these people will lose their way of life.*

Now these traditional ways of life, and even the very survival of forest people, is threatened. When outsiders move in to fell trees for timber and build roads, they bring diseases such as influenza that kill local people. Around the world, the numbers of forest people have fallen dramatically since outsiders arrived a few centuries ago.

▼ Traditional forest shelters are made of local materials such as bamboo poles lashed together with vines. Many shelters are raised on stilts to protect them against flooding after heavy rain.

Under the axe

The world's precious rainforests are now disappearing at a frightening speed. In fact, an area the size of several football pitches has been cut down in the few seconds it has taken you to read this paragraph.

A century ago, the world's tropical forests covered about twice the area they do today. So why are the forests being felled? One of the main reasons is for their valuable wood. Forest trees, such as teak and mahogany, yield a long-lasting timber called hardwood. This tough wood is used to make furniture, houses and many other items.

▼ It only takes a few minutes to cut down a mighty tree with a chainsaw, yet these trees take hundreds of years to grow.

▲ *This forest land in Southeast Asia has been cleared for mining.*

In some areas, rainforest trees are also being cut down by mining companies. The miners clear the land to drill for oil or dig for coal or precious metals such as gold and silver. Waste from the mines pollutes local rivers and kills the wildlife.

CLOSE TO HOME

Teak and mahogany are used to make luxury furniture for people in rich countries. Find out if there is any furniture made from hardwood in your home or visit a timber yard to look for it there.

Clearing the land

Logging and mining are not the only reasons for deforestation – the destruction of the rainforests. These beautiful forests are also cut down to clear land for farming and cattle-ranching and to make way for villages and dams.

Around the world, huge areas of leafy forest have been cleared to make space for plantations to grow crops such as rubber, sugar, palm oil, tea and coffee. When harvest time arrives, most of the crops are sold abroad rather than being used to feed the local people.

◄ This hillside in Dominica in the West Indies was once covered with dense forest of trees. The land was cleared to grow bananas.

CLOSE TO HOME

In places such as the Amazon, some forest land is burned and cleared to make pasture to raise beef cattle. Again, most of the meat is sold abroad. Much of the meat in beefburgers sold in fast-food restaurants in rich countries comes from cattle raised on cleared rainforest land.

▼ *This dam being built in Malaysia will be used to generate electricity. Once completed, water will build up behind the dam to flood and destroy a large area of forest.*

As the world's population grows, so more and more forest land is cleared to build towns and villages for people to live in. When big cities in tropical countries become overcrowded, governments encourage city folk to go and settle in the forest. However, many people find it hard to farm and make a living there.

After the loggers?

When the loggers move in, the peace of the forest is shattered. Forest animals flee as tree after tree is toppled. The logs are then loaded onto trucks or floated downriver to the sawmill, and the loggers move on.

When the loggers have gone, all that is left of the forest are sawn-off tree stumps and heaps of wood chips. Many of the young trees that have been spared by the chainsaw are broken and smashed. Without tree roots to anchor the soil, the earth becomes loose and crumbly. Heavy rain washes the soil away and causes landslides and floods.

▶ *Heavy rain is eroding (washing away) the soil from this hillside in Malaysia. Also, part of the rainforest has been flooded by Lake Kenyir.*

CLOSE TO HOME

Many of the foods found in your local supermarket come from the rainforest. Sugar, brazil nuts, peanuts, bananas, pineapples, lemons, avocados and cocoa for chocolate all originally grew wild in the rainforests. Now they are mostly grown on plantations on cleared forest land.

▼ *On cleared forest land, the water drains away more quickly without tree roots to suck up the moisture. This can leave the ground dry and bare. Fires commonly break out on cleared forest land, killing even more forest creatures.*

Much of the cleared land is then used for farming, but the forest soil is too thin and poor to nourish crops for long. After just three or four years, harvests dwindle. The farmers must move on, so new patches of rainforest have to be logged and cleared.

Wildlife in danger

When rainforests are cut down, the wildlife that lives there is threatened. Without trees, birds and other animals have no shelter. Without food, many creatures starve to death. Some forest animals are also killed by fires or hunted for their meat.

Many forest animals and plants are found only in one small part of the rainforest. If too much of their home is destroyed, they may become extinct, which means they die out altogether so that no more of their kind are left on Earth.

◀ *Mountain gorillas are found in the high, misty forests of Central Africa. They are hunted by poachers, and so much of their forest has been cut down that they are now rare.*

Experts fear that up to 50 different rainforest animals and plants are now becoming extinct every day because of the effects of deforestation. Many of these are insects and other small creatures. Scientists think that some types of animals and plants are dying out before they have even been identified.

CLOSE TO HOME

Rainforest people have used local plants for medicine for centuries. Now doctors in rich countries are using them, too. Fruit from the African sausage tree is now used to treat skin problems. The papaya from South America is used to treat stomach complaints.

▲ Tigers once roamed free through the huge forests of India and southern Asia. So much of the forest has now been lost that tigers are now listed as an endangered species.

Warming up

The destruction of the rainforests affects much more than just the local wildlife. It is also changing the balance of gases in the atmosphere, which is causing Earth's climate to get warmer.

Felled forests can no longer absorb carbon dioxide or top up oxygen levels. Instead, when trees are burned they release more carbon dioxide into the atmosphere. The gas forms a barrier that traps the Sun's rays near Earth's surface, which is causing the world's weather to get warmer. This process is known as global warming.

▼ Burning the rainforests increases levels of carbon dioxide in the air, which is causing Earth's climate to warm up.

Rising sea levels will threaten low-lying countries such as Holland, shown here. Whole island nations, such as the Maldives in the Indian Ocean, may become submerged.

If global warming continues, the ice in the polar regions may start to melt. This will cause sea levels to rise, bringing danger of flooding to coasts and islands around the world. Meanwhile, felled rainforests no longer soak up moisture from the soil and release it to form clouds that bring rain to surrounding regions. Some parts of the tropics have become much drier since neighbouring rainforests have been destroyed.

▼ The melting of the ice caps covering the polar regions would release a vast quantity of water.

Saving the forests

In the late twentieth century, forest people began to protest at the continued destruction of their homelands. They met with the governments of their countries and with representatives from nations around the world to discuss how the rainforests could be saved.

◀ *This young girl is protesting against logging in the Philippines, where floods made worse by deforestation have killed more than 8000 people.*

Rainforest countries are mostly poor. Logging, mining and other activities bring in useful cash, but there are other ways of making money from the forests without cutting them down. Fruits, nuts, medicinal plants and crops, such as rubber, can be harvested and sold without harming the trees.

Some parts of the rainforest have been turned into wildlife parks or reserves, where the animals and plants are protected. Tourists visiting these places bring in much-needed cash. In some rainforests, tree-cutting is now carefully managed. Selected trees or narrow strips of forest are cut, then the forest is allowed to grow back. Foresters plant young seedlings that will grow into mighty trees in years to come.

▲ At the Earth Summit in Brazil in 1992, forest people demanded a say in all new plans for their rainforest, such as logging, mines and dams.

LOOK CLOSER

Some forest creatures have been saved from extinction by being bred in zoos and parks. They include a monkey called the golden lion tamarin from South America, shown here. If the breeding programme is successful, the young animals can later be released in the wild in the remaining pockets of rainforest.

How can we help?

Rainforests make the world a better place. They help to keep the air rich in oxygen and bring rain to the surrounding regions. Just as rainforests affect us, so we can all help to save them. There are many practical ways in which everyone can help.

◀ *When your family buys wood products, try to find out where the wood comes from. This Forest Stewardship Council logo tells you the wood comes from properly managed forests.*

Some of the timber cut from rainforests is used to make beautiful furniture, but much is pulped to make paper for newspapers, magazines and packages – all products that are soon thrown away. Everyone can help by recycling paper so that it can be used again. This will help to save trees.

▶ *These children are recycling used paper.*

Help save the forests by supporting a charity that works with rainforest people or a campaign group such as Greenpeace, Friends of the Earth or the World Wildlife Fund. These organisations work to protect rainforests around the world. Some have schemes through which you can sponsor (send money to support) your favourite rainforest animal.

▼ *The trade in endangered animals, such as these parrots, is now illegal.*

▲ *Bonobos live in the rainforests of Africa. These peaceful apes are among the world's most intelligent animals. They are now endangered due to the loss of their forest home. Wildlife organisations have sponsorship schemes that help remarkable creatures like these survive in the wild.*

Rare plants, such as orchids, and animals, such as parrots, are sometimes collected from the wild and sold in rich countries. People buy them in pet shops, garden centres or on the Internet, which adds to their risk of extinction. If your family is thinking of buying tropical plants or pets, check that they have not been collected from the wild.

Forest projects

The rainforests may be far away, but you can bring them a little closer by growing a mini rainforest in a bottle! You can also use the same techniques scientists use in rainforests to identify the animals and plants in your local wood.

▲ *This scientist from the World Wildlife Fund is studying ferns in the forests of Madagascar.*

IDENTIFYING FOREST ANIMALS AND PLANTS

Scientists sometimes use a square frame called a quadrat to study forest wildlife. You can make a quadrat with eight pegs, a tape measure and some string. Ask an adult to help for safety.

1. Choose a patch of woodland soil, and put two pegs in the ground 1m apart. Run string between the pegs. Add more pegs and string to mark out a patch of ground 1m square.

2. Measure the midpoints of each side, and mark them with four more pegs. Run string between them to divide your frame into four equal parts.

3. Use a guide to local wildlife to identify all the types of plants growing inside the quadrat. Make a note of the numbers of each type. You could draw a chart to show your findings.

▶ *These children are investigating the wildlife found around a tree in Wareham Forest, Great Britain.*

RAINFOREST IN A BOTTLE

To make a mini rainforest you will need a large glass or transparent plastic bottle or a jar with a lid, a few small tropical house plants, potting compost, gravel and a trowel.

1. Use the trowel to line the bottom of the jar with gravel. Then add a deep layer of potting compost on top of the gravel.

2. Make holes in the soil for the plants with your trowel and gently lower the plants in. Firm the soil around the bottom of the plants.

3. Water the plants or mist them with a plant spray. Then seal the bottle or jar with a top or lid. You will not need to water your mini rainforest often because the plants will recycle the moisture inside.

CONSERVATION GROUPS

World Wildlife Fund (WWF)
Panda House, Weyside Park
Godalming, Surrey GU7 1XR
Website: www.wwf.org

Friends of the Earth
26–28 Underwood Street
London N1 7JQ
Website: www.foe.co.uk

Greenpeace
Canonbury Villas, London N1 2PN
Website: www.greenpeace.org

RAINFOREST WEBSITES

Animals of the rainforest: www.animalsoftherainforest.org

Rainforest Action Network: www.ran.org/kids_action

Rainforest diversity: www.forest.org

Enchanted Learning rainforest: www.enchantedlearning.com/subjects/rainforests

Animal Planet: www.animal.discovery.com

BBC's natural history website: www.bbc.co.uk/nature

National Geographic: www.nationalgeographic.com

Forest factfile

• Fifty different types of plants, including ferns, vines and orchids, have been identified growing on a single tree in the Amazon rainforest.

• Tall trees in tropical rainforests stand about 50m high – that's as high as a ten-storey building.

• Some parts of the Amazon rainforest receive over 1000 cm of rain each year. These are some of the wettest places on Earth.

• Experts have counted over 200 different types of tree in a tiny patch of tropical forest just 0.1 hectare in area.

• Scientists estimate that a total area of rainforest the size of Switzerland is being cut down each year.

• Many rare rainforest creatures are now protected by laws in their own countries. They include gorillas, orang-utans, tigers and Southeast Asian rhinos.

• It is against the law to pick plants or disturb animals in rainforest reserves and parks.

Glossary

Canopy
The dense, leafy layer found high above the ground in rainforests, formed by the interlocking branches of trees.

Carbon dioxide
A gas in the atmosphere that animals give off as they breathe and that plants absorb.

Climate
The regular pattern of weather in a certain area.

Deforestation
The cutting down and clearing of the rainforest.

Emergent
A tall tree that sticks up above the canopy in a rainforest.

Equator
An imaginary line running around the middle of Earth, at the widest point.

Extinction
When a particular type of plant or animal dies out altogether, so that no more of the same kind is left on Earth.

Global warming
The warming effect caused by certain gases, called greenhouse gases, in the atmosphere. These gases, which include carbon dioxide, trap the Sun's heat and send it back to Earth, where it warms the planet's surface.

Oxygen
A gas in the atmosphere that plants give off and that all animals need to breathe.

Species
A particular type of plant or animal such as the orang-utan, whose scientific name is *Pongo pygmaeus*.

Storeys
The vertical layers of life in a rainforest, from the tips of the tallest trees down to ground level.

Temperate zones
The cooler areas of Earth found north and south of the tropics.

Tropics
The regions found on either side of the Equator where the climate is hot all year round.

Understorey
The gloomy layer below the canopy in a rainforest, where there is hardly any light.

Index